Favorite Pets

Hamsters

by Derek Zobel

BLASTOFF!
Beginners

BELLWETHER MEDIA
MINNEAPOLIS, MN

Blastoff! Beginners are developed by literacy experts and educators to meet the needs of early readers. These engaging informational texts support young children as they begin reading about their world. Through simple language and high frequency words paired with crisp, colorful photos, Blastoff! Beginners launch young readers into the universe of independent reading.

Blastoff! Universe ★

Reading Level — Grade K

BLASTOFF! READERS — Grades 1-3

BLASTOFF! DISCOVERY — Grade 4

Sight Words in This Book 🔍

a	from	look	the	to
and	him	make	their	
are	in	many	them	
at	is	on	there	
day	it	play	they	
eat	like	run	this	

This edition first published in 2021 by Bellwether Media, Inc.

No part of this publication may be reproduced in whole or in part without written permission of the publisher. For information regarding permission, write to Bellwether Media, Inc., Attention: Permissions Department, 6012 Blue Circle Drive, Minnetonka, MN 55343.

Library of Congress Cataloging-in-Publication Data

Names: Zobel, Derek, 1983- author.
Title: Hamsters / by Derek Zobel.
Description: Minneapolis, MN : Bellwether Media, Inc., 2021. | Series: Blastoff! Beginners: Favorite pets | Includes bibliographical references and index. | Audience: Ages PreK-2 | Audience: Grades K-1
Identifiers: LCCN 2020007105 (print) | LCCN 2020007106 (ebook) | ISBN 9781644873168 (library binding) | ISBN 9781681038032 (paperback) | ISBN 9781681037790 (ebook)
Subjects: LCSH: Hamsters as pets--Juvenile literature. | Hamsters--Juvenile literature.
Classification: LCC SF459.H3 Z632 2021 (print) | LCC SF459.H3 (ebook) | DDC 636.935/6--dc23
LC record available at https://lccn.loc.gov/2020007105
LC ebook record available at https://lccn.loc.gov/2020007106

Editor: Amy McDonald   Designer: Jeffrey Kollock

Printed in the United States of America, North Mankato, MN.

Table of Contents

Pet Hamsters!

Spin, run, play! Hamsters make fun pets!

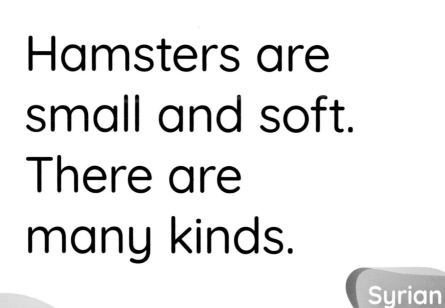

Hamsters are small and soft. There are many kinds.

Syrian

Chinese

Campbell's dwarf

Care

Hamsters live in cages. Cages need **bedding**. It keeps hamsters warm.

bedding

Hamsters build **nests**. They sleep in them.

nest

Hamsters
eat seeds.
They drink
from a bottle.

seeds

bottle

13

Hamsters like to **chew**. It keeps their teeth short.

chewing

Life with Hamsters

Hamsters play at night. They sleep in the day.

Hamsters
chew on toys.
They run
on wheels.

wheel

This hamster
is in a ball.
Look at him run!

Hamster Facts

Pet Hamster Supplies

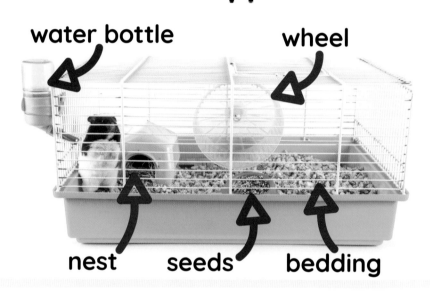

water bottle

wheel

nest

seeds

bedding

Hamster Toys

ball

chew toys

wheel

Glossary

bedding

small, soft
pieces of wood

chew

to bite with
teeth

nests

places where
animals rest
and sleep

To Learn More

ON THE WEB

FACTSURFER

Factsurfer.com gives you a safe, fun way to find more information.

1. Go to www.factsurfer.com.

2. Enter "pet hamsters" into the search box and click ○.

3. Select your book cover to see a list of related content.

Index

The images in this book are reproduced through the courtesy of: Kuttelvaserova Stuchelova, front cover; ZaZa Studio, p. 3; irin-k, p. 4; IhorL, pp. 4-5; TanyaKim, pp. 6-7; Olena Kurashova, p. 6; David Pegzlz, p. 7 (Chinese); Hintau Aliaksei, p. 7 (Campbell's dwarf); B. sunisa, pp. 8, 23 (bedding); Fantom_rd, pp. 8-9; RaquelVizcaino, pp. 10-11; Ermak Oksana, p. 12; Kristi Blokhim, pp. 12-13; Oleksandr Lytvynenko, p. 14; Olga Pleshakova, pp. 14-15; Montree Sanyos, pp. 16-17; Juniors Bildarchiv GmbH/ Alamy, p. 18; chaiyawat chaidet, pp. 18-19; Africa Studio, pp. 20-21; Martin Lisner, p. 22 (isolated); vladimirzahariev, p. 22 (ball); Arco Images GmbH/ Alamy, p. 22 (chew toys); AlexKalashnikov, p. 22 (wheel); Riepina Vadyslava, p. 23 (chew); dlugoska, p. 23 (nest).